The American Revolution

Christi E. Parker, M.A.Ed.

Table of Contents

What is the American Revolution?

The settlers in the original 13 colonies did not have many weapons. But, they had many reasons to fight a war. Great Britain was ruling them unfairly. They wanted to be free to govern themselves. To become free, they knew they would have to fight.

The colonists marched into battle and won the Revolutionary War. This war changed the lives of everyone. A new country was formed with a new type of **government**.

▼ Battle in Boston during the Revolution

▼ The American Revolution was fought to control the British colonies in America.

Why Did the War Begin?

Before the American Revolution, Great Britain fought in the French and Indian War. The colonists helped the British fight. They hoped the king would give them more land in America. Instead, Great Britain gave the land to the American Indians. This made the colonists angry.

Then, King George III sent soldiers to the colonies. The king charged the colonists taxes to pay for the soldiers. The colonists did not think they should have to pay taxes.

British Tax Stamp

King George III

The First to Die

British soldiers in the Boston Massacre shot Crispus Attucks. Attucks was a runaway slave.

Colonists did not have **representation** (rep-ri-zen-TAY-shun) in the British **Parliament** (PAR-luh-muhnt). Parliament was the part of the British government where laws were passed.

Parliament put a tax on stamps, sugar, and other goods. Some colonists **protested** these taxes. In Boston, a mob **taunted** (TAWNT-ed) a group of British soldiers. The British then fired on the mob. Five colonists were killed. The colonists called this shooting the "Boston Massacre" (MAS-uh-kuhr).

Propaganda

Paul Revere drew a picture of the Boston Massacre. But, it was not accurate. It showed the British soldiers firing on many colonists. It did not show what the colonists had done to make the British soldiers fire their guns.

More Trouble

Great Britain issued the Tea Act. This act put a tax on tea. A group of colonists dressed up as American Indians and went to Boston Harbor. They threw tea from three ships into the water. This was called the Boston Tea Party.

King George III punished the colonists by closing Boston Harbor. The colonists had to pay for the tea that was destroyed. King George sent warships into Boston Harbor. The colonists were forced to house British soldiers. The colonists really disliked these "Intolerable (in-TOL-uhr-uh-buhl) Acts."

Tea Parties Everywhere

Boston was not the only town to have a tea party. Colonists in New York and Annapolis, Maryland, also threw tea overboard to show their anger over the new taxes.

The colonists held a **Continental** (kon-tuh-NEN-tuhl) **Congress** in Philadelphia. This Congress sent a letter to King George III to protest the Intolerable Acts. The Continental Congress asked the colonists to **boycott** British goods and to prepare to fight.

▼ **Handbill urging boycott of British goods**

[January, 1770]

WILLIAM JACKSON,
an IMPORTER; at the
BRAZEN HEAD,
North Side of the TOWN-HOUSE,
and *Oppoſite the Town-Pump,* in
Corn-hill, BOSTON.

It is deſired that the SONS and DAUGHTERS of *LIBERTY*, would not buy any one thing of him, for in ſo doing they will bring Diſgrace upon *themſelves*, and their *Poſterity*, for *ever* and *ever*, AMEN.

Uniting the Colonies

Like the snake in this drawing, the colonists needed to join together to survive.

Marching Into Battle

British General Thomas Gage was sent to Boston to locate all the colonists' guns and supplies. Paul Revere and the **Sons of Liberty** were ready. They jumped on their horses to warn the colonists that the British were coming. Colonists, called **minutemen**, were prepared to fight as soon as they got the warnings.

The British soldiers and the colonial **militia** met in Lexington, Massachusetts. No one knows who fired the first shot. Eight colonists were killed and only one British soldier was hurt. This was called the "shot heard 'round the world" because this battle started the American Revolution.

▼ Paul Revere's famous ride

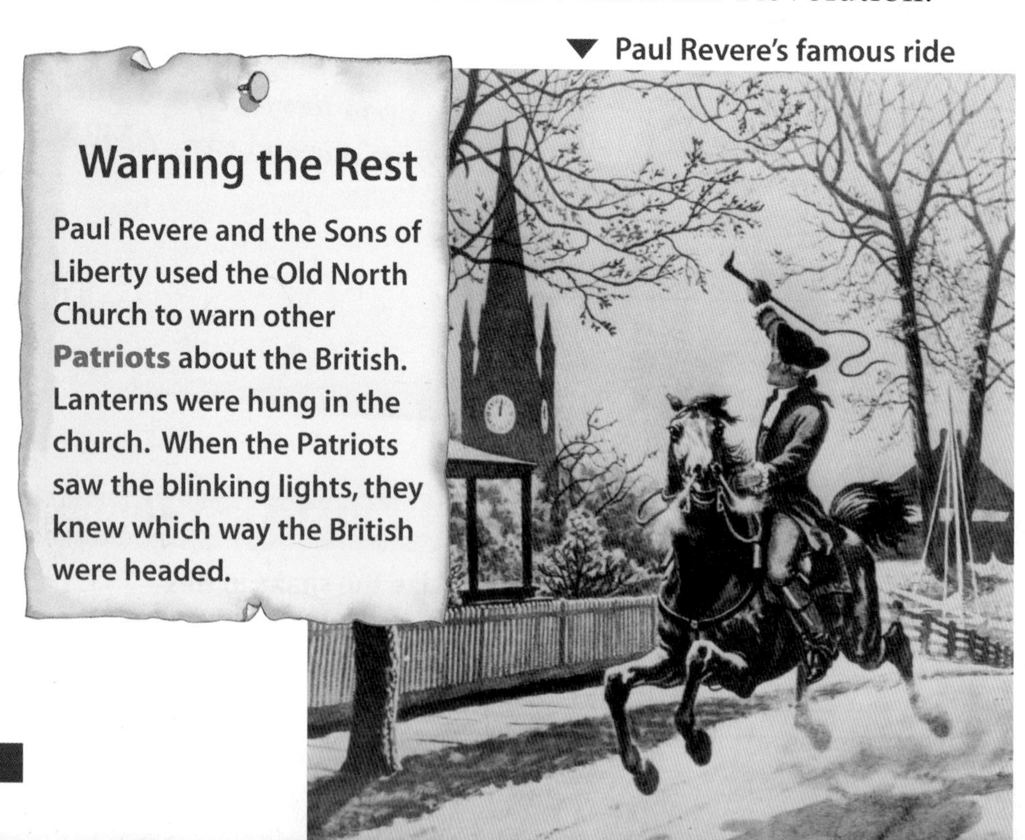

Warning the Rest

Paul Revere and the Sons of Liberty used the Old North Church to warn other **Patriots** about the British. Lanterns were hung in the church. When the Patriots saw the blinking lights, they knew which way the British were headed.

George Washington was named **commander** (kuh-MAN-duhr) of the **Continental Army**. His first job was to move the British Army out of Boston. His army surrounded Boston and forced the British soldiers into Canada.

Map of the region around Boston

Name Calling

The colonists made fun of the British by calling them "Lobster Backs." This was because their coats were red.

Fighting at the Battle of Lexington

Important Battles

▲ Washington's army crossing the Delaware River on December 25, 1776

On Christmas Day 1776, Washington made a major move to catch the **redcoats** off guard. The British had pushed his army back from New York to Pennsylvania. General Washington set out with his 2,500 troops to cross the Delaware River at night. The British were not expecting them. Washington's army landed in Trenton, New Jersey. They quickly captured the city.

Most people think of the Battle of Saratoga as the turning point in the war. General John Burgoyne, a British general,

▲ The surrender of General Burgoyne at Saratoga

wanted to capture Albany, New York. He crossed Lake Champlain and traveled down the Hudson River. He met colonial fighters in Saratoga, New York. The British lost the battle after fighting for a month.

This important victory by the colonial army showed France that the colonists could win the war. France decided to help the colonists. So, the French sent money and soldiers to the Continental Army.

▼ Soldiers at Valley Forge

Regaining Strength

George Washington and his men were very tired during the winter of 1777–1778. They spent the winter at Valley Forge. It was very cold there and they did not receive much food until early spring. Finally, they regained their strength and were ready to fight again.

Winning the War

The colonists did not have a strong navy. They only had private ships to fight Britain. France sent ships to help the colonists fight at sea.

John Paul Jones was the American commander at sea. He caught many British **merchant ships**. He even captured a British ship while his own ship was sinking!

Singing a Song

The song "Yankee Doodle" was sung by the British to make fun of the colonists. The colonists liked the tune, so they decided to use it as their theme song. The word *macaroni* in the song describes someone who is dressed up, not pasta.

▼ Sea battle during the Revolution

▲ French and colonial forces at the Battle of Yorktown

The First Submarine

The colonists tried to fight at sea with one of the first submarines. The "Turtle" was made of wood. Its job was to take a bomb and attach it to a British ship. The plan didn't work because the British saw the submarine.

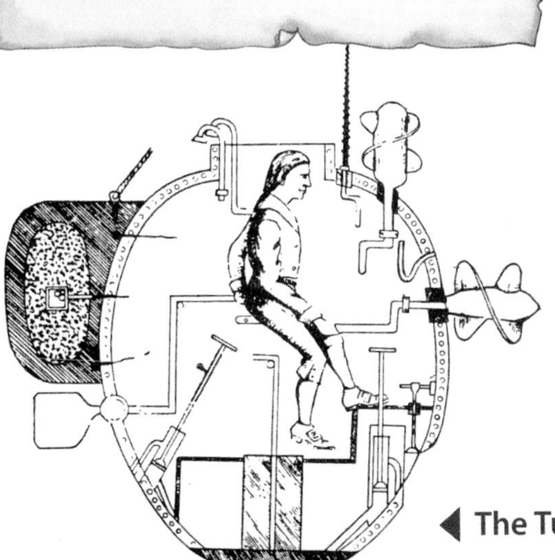

◀ The Turtle submarine

The last major battle of the war was at Yorktown, Virginia. It took place on October 11, 1781. General George Washington worked with the French to create a trap for British General Charles Cornwallis. The colonists and French set up a **blockade** at Yorktown. Cornwallis was not able to get his supplies. He **surrendered** (suh-REN-duhred) his armies and the war was over.

Spying for Information

Both the colonists and the British had spies. These spies hid secret messages. They took chances with their lives if they were caught.

Deborah Champion was a colonial spy. She easily rode past British soldiers because they thought a girl could do no harm. She would listen to what they were saying. Then, Deborah would give information to General George Washington.

▼ Nathan Hale being questioned by the British

Spying at All Costs

Nathan Hale was a spy for the colonists. He was caught while trying to leave New York. The British sent him to the gallows, where he was put to death.

Benedict Arnold was a spy, too. He was a colonial soldier, but he became upset when he was not promoted. He decided to become a spy for Britain. The British gave him money to pass secrets to them. When the colonists found out about him, he fled to London with his family.

Benedict Arnold

Friend or Foe?

Rachel Revere wrote a letter to her husband, Paul Revere, after his famous ride. She gave the letter and some money to her friend. He was supposed to deliver the letter to her husband. Her "friend" was actually a spy. He took the letter straight to the British.

▼ Rachel Revere's letter

my Dear by ~~Docr Church~~ I send a hundred & twenty five pounds
and beg you will take the best care of your self and not
attempt coming in to this town again and if I have
an opportunity of coming or sending out any thing or
any of the Children I shall do it pray keep up
your spirits and trust your self and us in the hands
of a good god who will take care of us tis all my
dependance for vain is the help of man adieu my
Love from your
affectionate R Revere

The People of the Revolution

Paul Revere was a Patriot and a member of the Sons of Liberty. This group protested taxes and the actions of King George III. Revere warned the minutemen that the British were coming. Though the British captured him, he was later set free.

George Washington was the commander of the Continental Army. He only won three major battles, but those battles changed the war. He later became the first president of the United States.

Will You Be King?

People liked George Washington so much that they wanted to make him king of America. He said, "No! We've had enough of kings!"

Molly Pitchers

Women helped the soldiers by carrying water for them in battle. They were given the nickname "Molly Pitcher." One woman even took her husband's place in battle after he was wounded!

General Charles Cornwallis fought for the British. Cornwallis was put in charge of the South after he captured the city of Charleston. He surrendered his army to Washington after losing the Battle of Yorktown.

General Cornwallis

Marquis de Lafayette was from France. He did not agree with Britain and its rule over the colonies. He bought his own ship and sailed to America. He fought with the colonists for no pay. Lafayette helped Washington win the Battle of Yorktown. He also convinced the French to help the colonists in the war.

Marquis de Lafayette

▼ Washington with some of the officers of the Colonial Army

Unique People During the War

A slave named Prince Estabrook was the only black man to fight at Lexington. Most black people were not allowed to join the Continental Army. Colonists worried that **slaves** would use the guns to fight for their own freedom. Later in the war, the government started to let slaves fight the British. Many blacks also fought for the British. The British promised them freedom after the war.

COMMON SENSE;

ADDRESSED TO THE

INHABITANTS

OF

AMERICA,

On the following interesting

SUBJECTS.

Thomas Paine

A Book to Unite

Thomas Paine was a Patriot who helped unite the colonists. He wrote a book called *Common Sense*. The book stated that America needed its own government. He wanted a government that could serve the people.

American Indians were often loyal to Great Britain. They were worried about the colonists taking their land after the war. Chief Joseph Brant led Iroquois (EAR-uh-kwoy) raids for the British in the New York area. The colonists called him "The Monster Brant."

On the other hand, the Oneida (oh-NI-duh) tribe fought with the colonists. They helped the colonists win the Battle of Saratoga. This battle is considered the turning point of the war.

Chief Joseph Brant

British Generals

Generals Charles Cornwallis and Thomas Gage both fought for the British. However, they were very different. General Cornwallis did not agree with the way the king treated the colonists, while General Gage helped enforce the Intolerable Acts.

Thomas Gage

Peace at Last

After the war, a **treaty** was written between Britain and the colonists. The Treaty of Paris was signed in France on September 3, 1783. Benjamin Franklin, John Jay, and John Adams helped lead the talks for the Americans.

The treaty stated that Great Britain had to accept the United States as its own country. Great Britain gave the United States land from the Atlantic Ocean to the Mississippi River. The United States stretched north and south from Canada to Florida.

The English had to remove all their troops from the United States. However, Great Britain was allowed to keep control of French Canada. The American government had to return any land that was taken during the war from British **Loyalists** (LOY-uh-lists). Great Britain was also permitted to continue to use the Mississippi River.

▼ The signing of the Treaty of Paris

Keeping the French Away

Benjamin Franklin, John Adams, and John Jay had orders to let the French be a part of the meetings in Paris. The three men were worried that the French would think the colonists were weak and needed to rely on them. So, they started the peace talks without French help.

Duplicate.

In the Name of the most Holy & undivided Trinity.

It having pleased the divine Providence to dispose the Hearts of the most Serene and most Potent Prince George the third, by the Grace of God, King of Great Britain, France & Ireland, Defender of the Faith, Duke of Brunswick and Lunenburg, Arch Treasurer and Prince Elector of the Holy Roman

The Treaty of Paris

John Adams

Fish for Everyone

The Treaty of Paris even outlined where the Americans could fish. They were only allowed to fish at certain British-controlled waterways.

After the War

Even though the colonists won the war, life in the new country was not easy. Many soldiers returned to their homes after the war and had no jobs or money.

The leaders of America had to decide how they wanted to set up their new country. As new laws were made, new problems started. Some farmers were concerned about the

▼ Washington's victory march through New York City

Getting a New President

The people knew they wanted George Washington as their first president. He did not actually take office until eight years after the war.

laws that were being made. Certain laws about voting meant that poor people like farmers could not help make important decisions.

Farmers were also angry about how much the government leaders got paid. Daniel Shay was a military officer during the war. After the war, he led unhappy farmers in **rebellions** (ri-BEL-yuns). He wanted to change the unfair laws. His actions were called Shay's Rebellion. Already the new Americans were making sure their country would be fair to all people.

What Happened to Shay?

Daniel Shay and the other rebels were captured and sentenced to death. The courts said they were not loyal to the government. They were later set free.

▼ The end of Shay's Rebellion

Glossary

blockade—a way of blocking the enemy so it cannot get in or out

boycott—refuse to buy or sell goods

commander—a person in charge of a group

Continental Army—the colonists who fought in the American Revolution

Continental Congress—the first government meeting in the United States

gallows—a place where people are hanged

government—a group of leaders that run a country and make laws

Loyalists—people in the colonies who were loyal to the king of England during the war

merchant ships—ships used to trade or sell items

militia—soldiers who only fight in emergencies

minutemen—people in the war that were ready to fight at a minute's notice

Parliament—the government of Great Britain

Patriots—people who fought for the colonies during the American Revolution

protested—objected or fought against something

rebellions—actions to show one's thoughts or anger

redcoats—a nickname given to British soldiers during the American Revolution

representation—standing in for someone or a group of people

slaves—people who were owned by other people and had no personal rights

Sons of Liberty—a group started by Samuel Adams to protest King George's actions

surrendered—gave up

taunted—teased or bothered

treaty—an agreement among countries